PowerKids Readers:

Big Cats
LEOPARDS

Elizabeth Vogel

The Rosen Publishing Group's
PowerKids Press™
New York

1

Published in 2002 by The Rosen Publishing Group, Inc.
29 East 21st Street, New York, NY 10010

First Edition

Book design: Michael Donnellan

Photo Credits: pp. 1, 15 © Telegraph Colour Library/FPG; p. 5 © Animals Animals/Gerard Lacz; p. 7 © Bob Jacobson/International Stock; p. 9 © Mark Newman/International Stock; p. 11 © Stan Osolinski/FPG International; pp. 13, 19 © A. Schmidecker/FPG International; pp.16, 17 © John Lambert/Artville Stock Images; p. 21 © Frank Grant/International Stock.

Vogel, Elizabeth.
  Leopards / Elizabeth Vogel.
    p. cm. — (Big cats)
  Includes bibliographical references (p.   ). and index.
  ISBN 0-8239-6019-6 (lib. bdg.)
  1. Leopard—Juvenile literature. [1. Leopard.]   I. Title.
QL737.C23 V636 2002
599.75'54—dc21

                                    00-013249

Manufactured in the United States of America

CONTENTS

Leopards are big cats
that have a mighty roar.

Leopards are big and strong. Leopards have long tails, too.

Adult leopards are big, but baby leopards are small. Baby leopards are called cubs.

All leopards have soft, beautiful fur. Their fur can be yellow, orange, or black.

Some leopards have only black fur. These leopards are called panthers.

Leopards also can have black spots and rings on their fur.

Leopards like to eat meat.
They eat monkeys
and baboons.

17

Leopard cubs learn a lot from their mothers. They learn how to hunt and what to eat.

Leopards can live
in different places.
Many leopards live
on mountaintops.

21

WORDS TO KNOW

baboon

cub

monkey

spots

Here are more books to read about leopards:

The Big Cats: Lions and Tigers and Leopards
by Jennifer Urquehart
National Geographic Society

Leopards
by Don Middleton
Rosen Publishing

To learn more about leopards, check out these Web sites:
www.discovery.com
http://home.iprimus.com.au/tigris/main.htm

23

INDEX

B
baboons, 16

C
cubs, 8, 18

F
fur, 10, 12, 14

H
hunt, 18

M
monkeys, 16
mountaintops, 20

P
panthers, 12

R
roar, 4

S
spots, 14

T
tails, 6

Word Count: 107

Note to Librarians, Teachers, and Parents

PowerKids Readers are specially designed to help emergent and beginning readers build their skills in reading for information. Simple vocabulary and concepts are paired with stunning, detailed images from the natural world around them. Readers will respond to written language by linking meaning with their own everyday experiences and observations. Sentences are short and simple, employing a basic vocabulary of sight words, as well as new words that describe objects or processes that take place in the natural world. Large type, clean design, and photographs corresponding directly to the text all help children to decipher meaning. Features such as a contents page, picture glossary, and index help children to get the most out of PowerKids Readers. They also introduce children to the basic elements of a book, which they will encounter in their future reading experiences. Lists of related books and Web sites encourage kids to explore other sources and to continue the process of learning.